Prayer request:
Dores ----
weather ---
Jein Anderson -
Jim Davidson -

Bob Anderson -- - Howard --
Blanche -
- Harvey -
Jackie Keller - daughter -
Judy gr - flubn,   1½ yr.
fragile -
Irma - housekeeper of

Stories Jesus Told
Leader Guide

Stories Jesus Told
Leader Guide

Stories Jesus Told Leader Guide
978-1-5018-8424-5
978-1-5018-8425-2 eBook

Stories Jesus Told
978-1-5018-8415-3
978-1-5018-8416-0 eBook

Stories Jesus Told DVD
978-1-5018-8417-7

GREG CAREY

STORIES

JESUS

TOLD

HOW TO READ
A PARABLE

LEADER GUIDE
by Randy Petersen

Abingdon Press / Nashville

Stories Jesus Told

LEADER GUIDE

Feb. 13 - Ted Pockman   U M H
Richelle - Jackie/Reller ＩＯＩ
Reller - IOV
Howard Schneider -
Pat - Dr. mon. eye -
IT Dept. - ==
Dorea - eye exam -
Nava -
Alesha =
Wisdom -
patience -
understanding -

Contents

JOHN & NANCY GARTH
DARYTON & BEV. BOOZER
JANUE MOFFIT
MARCIA McCLORAN
BETTY KOCH
DONIA COOK
DOLONAS MICHASON
JANE MANNIR
PAVLINE TAUSINO ?

Introduction

Jesus loved to tell stories. His parables generally involved everyday activities, common characters, and familiar relationships. He wasn't the only teacher in the ancient world to use parables, but he used them in unique ways, painting word-pictures of God's kingdom. Perhaps the most distinctive feature of these stories, according to author Greg Carey, is that "they challenge readers and hearers to think for themselves."

So don't expect Carey—or this leader guide, for that matter—to tell you what the parables mean. And that's not your job as a teacher or leader. This guide will help you bring your group into the parables of Jesus, filling out the context, but letting them experience these surprising stories and their lessons for themselves.

The questions and activities in this guide are designed to spark connections between those age-old stories and the modern lives of group members. Maybe you've never gone hunting for a lost sheep, but have you ever lost your keys? While some details may need explaining, the parables' impact transcends time.

In each parable, Carey urges us to look for the "hook"—which he defines as "that part of a parable where the story abandons conventional logic and jumps off the rails." These tales are full of surprises, head-scratchers, and hard left turns. Some Bible students can develop the bad habit of sanding down the rough edges of Scripture into familiar lessons. The stories of Jesus defy that practice.

People in your group may have questions like that, and they'll ask them if you encourage them to. Give them explicit permission to be as unconventional as Jesus was.

"A parable's hook challenges us to open our imaginations to the possibility that the things of God are not as we'd expect," Carey writes. "Parables with hooks refuse to wrap spiritual lessons in fancy paper and tie them up with a pretty bow. Parables challenge us to look one another in the eye, to explore the mystery of the kingdom together."

SESSIONS

The six sessions of this study guide correspond to the six chapters of *Stories Jesus Told* by Greg Carey:

- **Session 1—Divine Inefficiencies (Mark 4:1-20)**
  The Parable of the Sower shows God's message being scattered on good soil and bad alike. Isn't that wasteful? Come to think of it, aren't parables themselves rather inefficient? This opening session introduces us to the concept of parables, including why Jesus used them and how we can approach them.

- **Session 2—Funny Business (Matthew 20:1-16)**
  The Parable of the Workers in the Vineyard raises curious questions. While Jesus often drew his stories from the daily business of his hearers—fishing, farming, herding, and getting paid—it's seldom "business as usual." The Master Teacher routinely challenges our assumptions.

- *Session 3—Weddings Gone Awry (Matthew 22:1-14; 25:1-13)*
  The Parables of the Wedding Party and the Brides-maids are rooted in first-century culture, but each one has its surprises. And just when we think we get it, there's a new twist.

- *Session 4—Lawyers and Samaritans (Luke 10:25-37)*
  The Parable of the Good Samaritan is one of the best-known stories in the Bible, but most people get it wrong. This session digs into who these characters are and how this parable answers the question "Who is my neighbor?"

- *Session 5—Losing, Finding, Partying (Luke 15:1-32)*
  The Parable of the Prodigal Son is probably the next-best-known parable, but this presents challenges too. This session looks at all three main characters in that drama, and at the other two "lost and found" stories contained in Luke 15.

- *Session 6—A Reversal of Fortune (Luke 16:19-31)*
  Several of Jesus' parables deal with surprising turn-about. "The last shall be first," Jesus liked to say. The Rich Man and Lazarus is a great example, extending beyond the death of both characters. This session works to strip away the theological presuppositions that might keep us from reading this story on its own terms.

Each session contains the following elements:

- **Session Goals**
- **Biblical Foundations**—The key Scripture passages discussed in each chapter, drawn from the Common English Bible (CEB).

- **Chapter Summaries**—Key points from *Stories Jesus Told*.
- **Materials You Will Need**—Occasionally, an activity will require extra supplies.
- **Opening and Closing Activities**—These activities are generally simple and often discussion-based, but they serve to get a group connecting with the Scripture in a novel way.
- **Opening and Closing Prayers**—Suggested wording. Please make them your own, or substitute with your own words.
- **Bible Study and Book Discussion**—Questions that dig into the central Scripture passages for each lesson, as well as quotations from *Stories Jesus Told*.

We pray that this guide would help your group unpack the parables of Jesus in refreshing—and possibly surprising—ways.

Session 1

Divine Inefficiencies

SESSION GOALS

This session aims to help group members:

- Understand the role of parables in Jesus' teaching.
- Consider ways that we might read and interpret Jesus' parables in our day.
- Open up to the surprises and challenges of the parables.
- Reflect on the Parable of the Sower in particular, with its suggestion of "divine inefficiencies."

BIBLICAL FOUNDATIONS

Jesus began to teach beside the lake again. Such a large crowd gathered that he climbed into a boat there on the lake. He sat in the boat while the whole crowd was nearby on the shore.

He said many things to them in parables. While teaching them, he said, "Listen to this! A farmer went out to scatter seed. As he was scattering seed, some fell on the path; and the birds came and ate it. Other seed fell on rocky ground where the soil was shallow. They sprouted immediately because the soil wasn't deep. When the sun came up, it scorched the plants; and they dried up because they had no roots. Other seed fell among thorny plants. The thorny plants grew and choked the seeds, and they produced nothing. Other seed fell into good soil and bore fruit. Upon growing and increasing, the seed produced in one case a yield of thirty to one, in another case a yield of sixty to one, and in another case a yield of one hundred to one." He said, "Whoever has ears to listen should pay attention!"

When they were alone, the people around Jesus, along with the Twelve, asked him about the parables. He said to them, "The secret of God's kingdom has been given to you, but to those who are outside everything comes in parables. This is so that they can look and see but have no insight, and they can hear but not understand. Otherwise, they might turn their lives around and be forgiven.

"Don't you understand this parable? Then how will you understand all the parables? The farmer scatters the word. This is the meaning of the seed that fell on the path: When the word is scattered and people hear it, right away Satan comes and steals the word that was planted in them. Here's the meaning of the seed that fell on rocky ground: When people hear the word, they immediately receive it joyfully. Because they have no roots, they last for only a little while. When they experience distress or abuse because of the word, they immediately fall away. Others are like the seed scattered among the thorny plants. These are the ones who have heard the word; but the worries of this life, the false appeal of wealth, and the desire for more things break in and choke the word, and it bears no fruit. The seed scattered on good soil are those who hear the word and embrace it. They bear fruit, in one case a yield of thirty to one, in another case sixty to one, and in another case one hundred to one."

Mark 4:1-20

CHAPTER SUMMARY

The Parable of the Sower (sometimes called the Parable of the Soils) is a great place to start a study of these unique stories of Jesus. This is the first parable presented in Mark, which is generally considered the first Gospel written. In addition, this is one of the few parables where Jesus provides an interpretation. This passage even includes a discussion about *why* Jesus used parables.

In the story, God's word goes forth and gets different kinds of receptions—represented by the different soils. In *Stories Jesus Told*, Greg Carey points out an issue that many non-farmers might miss. Wouldn't a good farmer know where the good soil is? Why would he waste precious seed on non-receptive terrain? And what does that say about God? Is God "inefficient" in broadcasting his message even to those who won't be receptive?

Carey also relays a theory suggesting that the different types of soils represent specific people or groups that we meet in the Gospels. Jesus' opponents—the Pharisees and other leaders—were much like the hardened path. Could the rocky soil stand for Peter (whose very name means *rock*) in his tendency to sprout quickly in support of Jesus and then wither away? The thorny soil could be an apt image for the rich young man who hung onto his wealth rather than following Jesus.

Materials You Will Need

- Bibles (preferably Common English Bible)
- Video set up to play
- Paper and writing utensils for the closing activity

DURING THE SESSION

Opening Activity and Prayer (8-12 minutes)

After welcoming everyone, introduce yourself and the study, *Stories Jesus Told*. Explain that each of the six group sessions covers a chapter of the book, and you'll be dealing with chapter 1 today.

Invite each group member to give his or her name, along with an answer to this question: *What experience do you have with farming or gardening?*

Take your time with these introductions. Feel free to launch a follow-up question or two along the way. *Your parents ran a farm? Where was that? Oh, you're a gardener; what do you like to grow?* You might even ask some of the "experts," *What do you think is the most important factor for a successful garden: watering, a sunny location, regular weeding, or good soil?* (That will come in handy later.)

When those introductions conclude, open the study with prayer:

O Lord, we long to know what you want to teach us. Our hearts and mind are open to your truth. Instruct us, challenge us, surprise us, delight us as we come before your word today.

Video Introduction (12 minutes)

Play the video for Session 1 of *Stories Jesus Told*.

Afterward, ask the group what they thought of the ideas presented there. What grabbed them? What was new to them? What questions do they have?

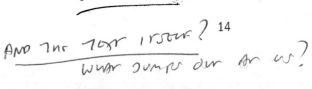

Bible Study and Book Discussion (25 minutes)

Invite the group to turn to Mark 4 in their Bibles. Ask someone to read verses 1-3 aloud. Ask: **vv. 1-9**

- What's the setting for this chapter?
- Imagine yourself in that crowd. How do you feel? What do you see, hear, or smell?
- Why do you think he tells a story about a farmer, rather than, say, a rabbi or a lawyer?

Invite someone else to read verses 4-9. Ask the group to repeat the main parts of the story. As much as you can, make this visual. Maybe you point to the four corners of the room you're in. Or maybe certain people in your group represent different soils. Make sure they understand what happens in each different type of soil (and if you can hark back to your farming/gardening conversation in the introduction time, so much the better). Ask:

- When Jesus asks for attention from "anyone who has ears to listen," what do you think he means? Is this just a generic "Listen up," or is he referring to something deeper?

Invite someone to read verses 10-12. Ask: **vv. 10**

- How does the scene change in these verses? Who is Jesus talking with?
- According to Matthew, these disciples asked him why he taught in parables. How would you sum up his response?
- What's the difference between the disciples and those "outside"?

Read the following selection from Greg Carey's book:

cf. Ps. 19 — 4 or
main com 2 opposing
Conclusion !

Why?

Isa. 6:9, 10

1 Con. 2:14-16
2 Con. 2:14-16

What Does
This Say
About θ ?
About us ?

The disciples ask Jesus why he speaks in parables, and Jesus replies that he uses parables so that those outside will fail to understand. The parables, then, discriminate between insiders and outsiders. Insiders should understand what Jesus means, but outsiders will find the parables frustrating or confusing.

This passage may pose a problem for many of us modern readers. For one thing, we've often heard that Jesus used parables to help people understand his message. We're used to thinking of parables like nifty teaching illustrations that make a point simple, or if not simple, then at least easy to understand. But Mark says that parables do not work that way. He says they raise barriers that prevent outsiders from understanding. Ask:

- Does this pose a problem for you, as Carey suggests?
- How do you understand what Jesus says about seeing without insight or hearing without understanding?

11/16

Invite someone to read Mark 4:13-20. Review this content as you did before, with the four corners of the room or four groups of people. Of course, now you have the meaning and not just the soils. Then ask:

- According to these verses, what sorts of difficulties keep people from receiving God's message?
- Have you encountered any of these difficulties in your own experience or in others? When? How?
- How does God's message "bear fruit"? How have you seen this happen?

In his book, Greg Carey points out something that many readers miss—and he made this the title of this chapter—"Divine Inefficiencies." Read the following excerpt to your group:

Divine Inefficiencies

When it comes to the Parable of the Soils, we rarely pause to investigate one detail: the sower/farmer casts seed on a path, on shallow soil, and among thorns. What reasonable farmer would cast most of his seed on unpromising soil?

To a modern reader, it seems our farmer is a model of inefficiency. . . . A sower who scatters seed in unpromising soil opens us to wonder. Does God scatter the good news even in the most unpromising places, regardless of the likely outcomes? Perhaps God is more generous than we might imagine, willing to "waste" the divine resources even among the most unlikely of us. That would be good news indeed.

Ask:

- What do you think of that? Is this parable telling us something about the "reckless love" of God? Or is there some other explanation?
- How does that make you feel, if God is willing to scatter his message even to those unlikely to respond?

Closing Activity and Prayer (8 minutes)

Refer to the theory in Carey's book that the different types of soils represent specific people or groups that we meet in the Gospels.

- Hardened path = Jesus' opponents—the Pharisees and other leaders.
- Rocky soil = Peter, sprouting quickly to support Jesus and then withering away.
- Thorny soil = the "rich young ruler," or perhaps Herod or Pilate.
- Good soil?

Ask them to take a piece of paper (hand out paper and pens as necessary) and write in the four corners: Path, Rock, Thorns, and Good Soil.

Suggest that they write down times in their lives when they have fit those descriptions: Resistant, Inconsistent, Distracted, or Productive. Give them a couple of minutes to think and pray about this. Then offer two questions:

- What can you do or say in the coming week to help God's message take root and grow in you?
- How can you pray for this in the coming week?

Close in prayer:

Our Lord, thank you for sending your message into our lives. We pray for ourselves as we represent the different soils in Jesus' parable. Sometimes we have received your word and we are growing, and we thank you for this, confident that you will continue your good work in us. But also help us as we struggle like the difficult soils. Keep sending your message to us, and give us strength. Work a miracle in us. Amen.

Session 2

Funny Business

SESSION GOALS

This session aims to help group members:

- Learn two ways to look at the Parable of the Workers in the Vineyard.
- Consider their own response to God's grace.
- Consider their own responsibilities in applying God's justice.
- Open up to the various surprises that Jesus' parables offer.

BIBLICAL FOUNDATIONS

"The kingdom of heaven is like a landowner who went out early in the morning to hire workers for his vineyard. After he agreed with the workers to pay them a denarion, he sent them into his vineyard.

"Then he went out around nine in the morning and saw others standing around the marketplace doing nothing. He said to them, 'You also go into the vineyard, and I'll pay you whatever is right.' And they went.

"Again around noon and then at three in the afternoon, he did the same thing. Around five in the afternoon he went and found others standing around, and he said to them, 'Why are you just standing around here doing nothing all day long?'

"'Because nobody has hired us,' they replied.

"He responded, 'You also go into the vineyard.'

"When evening came, the owner of the vineyard said to his manager, 'Call the workers and give them their wages, beginning with the last ones hired and moving on finally to the first.' When those who were hired at five in the afternoon came, each one received a denarion. Now when those hired first came, they thought they would receive more. But each of them also received a denarion. When they received it, they grumbled against the landowner, 'These who were hired last worked one hour, and they received the same pay as we did even though we had to work the whole day in the hot sun.'

"But he replied to one of them, 'Friend, I did you no wrong. Didn't I agree to pay you a denarion? Take what belongs to you and go. I want to give to this one who was hired last the same as I give to you. Don't I have the right to do what I want with what belongs to me? Or are you resentful because I'm generous?' So those who are last will be first. And those who are first will be last."

Matthew 20:1-16

CHAPTER SUMMARY

There are two very different interpretations of the Parable of the Workers in the Vineyard made by two different groups of readers. We might call them the "grace camp" and the "justice camp."

Those in the grace camp tend to see this story as a spiritual statement, along the lines of the apostle Paul's theology of grace. Those who have worked in the vineyard all day are like people who trust their good works to save them. They grumble about those who receive God's grace by faith, and perhaps late in life, after decades of unrighteous living. The parable is expressing God's desire to show grace to all.

Those in the justice camp put the focus on earth rather than heaven. This parable shows God's desire to provide for the basic needs of all people, whether gainfully employed or not. Carey notes, "Jesus framed his parables around such mundane human matters because issues like status, labor, and relationships were important to him." The fact that the last-hired were first-paid is in keeping with the upside-down nature of God's kingdom.

The double-reading of this parable helps us see two possible definitions of the "kingdom of heaven." Many look forward to a future kingdom, and so they see issues of eternal salvation in this and other parables. But, with a reference to the familiar wording of the Lord's Prayer, Carey points out that "God's kingdom happens when God's will is done." We can see the kingdom as both future and *now*.

Materials You Will Need

- Bibles (preferably Common English Bible)
- Video set up to play
- Index cards (or paper) and writing utensils for the closing activity

DURING THE SESSION

Opening Activity and Prayer (6-10 minutes)

Welcome folks as they arrive. If there's time for small talk, ask people about their daily work. What do they do? How are things at work? And don't neglect homemakers, retirees, or students—they're working too. This is a great way for people to get to know each other better.

As you officially begin, remind the group that you're studying the parables of Jesus, following the book *Stories Jesus Told* by Greg Carey. Explain that each of the six group sessions covers a chapter of the book, and you'll be dealing with chapter 2 today, about the story of the workers in the vineyard.

Since the parable involves getting paid for work done, ask the group: *What was the first job you ever had that you got paid for?*

Depending on their responses, you may want to follow up with questions like these: *Do you remember how it felt to get paid? What did you do with the money? Did it seem like a lot or a little? Did you feel you deserved it, or did you deserve more?*

When that conversation winds down, open the Bible-study portion of the meeting with prayer:

Lord, teach us today through your Scriptures. Help us to see with new eyes. Give us the courage to think new thoughts. Fill our hearts and minds with your holy energy. Amen.

Video Introduction (12 minutes)

Play the video for Session 2 of *Stories Jesus Told*.

Afterward, ask the group what they thought of the ideas presented there. What grabbed them? What was new to them? What questions do they have?

Bible Study and Book Discussion (30 minutes)

Invite the group to turn to Matthew 20 in their Bibles. (If the people don't have Bibles or a Bible app on their phone, you might have extra Bibles on hand, or print out the Matthew 20 text separately.) Have someone read verses 1-2 aloud. Ask:

- *Who* are the characters in this story?
- *When* did this happen?
  "Early in the morning" is all it says, but given the other times in the story, we might guess it was around 6 a.m.

- *Where* is this happening?
  Note that we're not given a place. Presumably it occurred wherever people went to get hired. Verse 3 identifies it as the "marketplace."

- *What* were the terms of the agreement?
  Note that a denarion (or denarius) was generally considered the wage for a day of labor. In the book, Carey points out that we don't know if this was enough to support a family or just an individual, but it was considered a fair wage for a day's work.

Have someone read verses 3-7. As much as possible, visualize these five groups of workers by breaking your group into five parts. "You're the original workers. You came on at 9 a.m. Etc." Ask:

- How has the agreement changed?
- Do you think it's significant that these workers were "doing nothing" or just "standing around"?
- If you had never heard or read this parable before, what would you expect this pay scale to be? Who would get paid what?

Have someone read verses 8-15. Ask:

- Who was paid first?
- Do you think this order is significant? How? Why?
- What did they get paid?
- If you were one of these workers, how would you feel?

Depends on what group you're in, right? (Use the five divisions you made earlier. *You one-hour workers* get paid a full day's wage, so *you whole-day people* think you're getting twelve times that.)

- How did the master respond to the grumbling?
- How do you feel about that response?

Let's turn our minds to interpretation. Ask the group to look back at the first few words of the chapter. This parable is about *the* kingdom of heaven. But what does that mean? You may want to review Carey's discussion of this term as opposed to "the kingdom of God," used by Mark and Luke. The Jews had deep reverence for the name of God and often replaced it with other terms, like "heaven." This Gospel is the most Jewish of the four, so it makes sense that, as Carey suggests, "Matthew probably prefers 'kingdom of heaven' out of reverence for the divine name."

Some people in your group might assume that "kingdom of heaven" refers to our heavenly future, and Carey acknowledges that it "often seems to point beyond the present moment," but that's not the whole story. "Matthew also uses 'kingdom of heaven' in ways that have here-and-now connotations," says Carey—such as the Lord's Prayer.

Ask your group:

- What does the Lord's Prayer say about God's kingdom? Is it future or present? Is it heavenly or earthly?

SUBJ.
12 CQ.

Funny Business

You may wish to share this line from the book: "God's kingdom happens when God's will is done. That can be on earth and in heaven, now or in the future."

Carey talks about two groups with different ways of interpreting this parable. He calls them "the grace camp" and "the justice camp." The grace camp thinks the parable is about how we get into God's heavenly kingdom. The justice camp thinks it's about how we treat people on earth. Ask:

- If you had to choose, which "camp" would you be in? Do you think this parable is about eternal grace or about earthly justice?
- How would those in the "grace camp" interpret this parable? Who are the all-day workers and who are the one-hour workers? And, assuming the landowner is in the God role, what does God do for them?
- Now how would the "justice camp" view the parable? Who do the all-day workers represent—and the one-hour workers? What does God give them?

Share what Carey wrote:

> Grace camp interpretations emphasize the landowner's generosity, while the justice camp stresses that each worker receives a fair wage. Both interpretations show that God's justice gives everyone what she or he needs, but they perceive human need differently. Does the parable primarily involve spiritual salvation, or does the kingdom of heaven bear upon our material conditions as well?

Ask:

- Does this help you decide between the two?
- Could both be right?

25

Read verse 16, the end of this parable, aloud. Ask the group to look at the end of Matthew 19. What do we see there? Are there any questions there that this parable answers? Just the rich young ruler, who thought he deserved eternal life because of his years of good living, and the disciples, who said they had given up a lot to follow Jesus.

When the landowner pays the one-hour workers first, that might be the key moment of this parable, according to Carey. Share what he wrote:

> The parable's sharp edge lies with that "hook," a reversal in expectation. It's not simply that in God's reign everyone receives enough. It's that Jesus proclaims a world in which our assumptions about standing in God's dominion are flipped upside-down. Those who think they're first had better think again!

Ask:

- How does this affect your opinion of this parable?

Closing Activity and Prayer (8 minutes)

Hand out index cards (or paper) and writing utensils (as needed). Ask them three questions:

- What does this parable inspire you to do?
- How should the church respond to this story?
- What could society learn from this parable?

Ask them to take a few minutes to think and pray about that and then answer at least one of those questions, and maybe all three.

If you have a few minutes remaining, invite people who

wish to share their responses to do so, but don't pressure anyone.

Then close in prayer:

Dear Lord, we thank you for your surprising generosity. We know you give us far more than we deserve. Help us to extend your generosity to others, sharing your love and sharing our resources. May you find pleasure as we receive your grace and work for justice. Amen.

Extra Activity (10-20 minutes)

If you have a longer time frame and an active group, you might add this activity early in the session. Divide into subgroups of five or six people. (If you have fewer than ten people in your whole group, they can all work together on this.)

The goal is to retell this parable in a modern setting. Don't worry about clever dialogue; we know the gist of the story. But choose a particular business that might hire people and negotiate terms. Have fun with it, but try to capture the main points of Jesus' story.

Take about three minutes to decide the structure and assign roles.

Take about five minutes to practice.

Then have each group "perform" it for the others.

Session 3

Weddings Gone Awry

SESSION GOALS

This session aims to help group members:

- Get to know these two "wedding parables" in Matthew.
- Take the invitation of God seriously in their own lives.
- Consider how they might be prepared for their future with Christ.

BIBLICAL FOUNDATIONS

Jesus responded by speaking again in parables: "The kingdom of heaven is like a king who prepared a wedding party for his son. He sent his servants to call those invited to the wedding party. But they didn't want to come. Again he sent other servants and said to them, 'Tell those who have been invited, "Look, the meal is all prepared. I've butchered the oxen and the fattened cattle. Now everything's ready. Come to the wedding party!"' But they paid no attention and went away—some to their fields, others to their businesses.

The rest of them grabbed his servants, abused them, and killed them.

"The king was angry. He sent his soldiers to destroy those murderers and set their city on fire. Then he said to his servants, 'The wedding party is prepared, but those who were invited weren't worthy. Therefore, go to the roads on the edge of town and invite everyone you find to the wedding party.'

"Then those servants went to the roads and gathered everyone they found, both evil and good. The wedding party was full of guests. Now when the king came in and saw the guests, he spotted a man who wasn't wearing wedding clothes. He said to him, 'Friend, how did you get in here without wedding clothes?' But he was speechless. Then the king said to his servants, 'Tie his hands and feet and throw him out into the farthest darkness. People there will be weeping and grinding their teeth.'

"Many people are invited, but few people are chosen."

Matthew 22:1-14

"At that time the kingdom of heaven will be like ten young bridesmaids who took their lamps and went out to meet the groom. Now five of them were wise, and the other five were foolish. The foolish ones took their lamps but didn't bring oil for them. But the wise ones took their lamps and also brought containers of oil.

"When the groom was late in coming, they all became drowsy and went to sleep. But at midnight there was a cry, 'Look, the groom! Come out to meet him.'

"Then all those bridesmaids got up and prepared their lamps. But the foolish bridesmaids said to the wise ones, 'Give us some of your oil, because our lamps have gone out.'

"But the wise bridesmaids replied, 'No, because if we share with you, there won't be enough for our lamps and yours. We have a better idea. You go to those who sell oil and buy some for yourselves.' But while they were gone to buy oil, the groom came. Those who were ready went with him into the wedding. Then the door was shut.

"Later the other bridesmaids came and said, 'Lord, lord, open the door for us.'

"But he replied, 'I tell you the truth, I don't know you.'

"Therefore, keep alert, because you don't know the day or the hour."

Matthew 25:1-13

CHAPTER SUMMARY

Late in Matthew's Gospel, Jesus' teachings turn toward future judgment. That's where we find two parables about weddings—the Wedding Party and the Bridesmaids.

The story of the Wedding Party (Matthew 22:1-14) starts out odd and ends bizarre. Guests refuse an invitation to a royal wedding and earn the king's violent wrath. Then invitations are sent out far and wide to a mixture of good and bad people who come to the party. One guest, however, is not wearing a suitable wedding garment, and he's thrown out.

This parable seems to connect with the tale of the Tenants in the previous chapter, in which the king's messengers are mistreated and even killed. Disrespect of the king deserves a violent backlash. Many see these parables as warnings to Jesus' enemies, the religious elite of Israel, who were ignoring God's invitation. Though the wedding-garment scene remains puzzling, it's another example of the "sifting" we find in several parables.

The Bridesmaids story seems to lack a hook, a surprise. From the start, half are called "wise" and the others "foolish," so we can guess what happens. The foolish ones are unprepared for the groom's delay. Some interpreters suggest ways the wise ones might have proved their wisdom by sharing oil or sharing light, but this might merely complicate a simple story.

This fits squarely in Matthew's "future" section, but it

seems to focus on how Jesus' followers deal with the delay of Jesus' return.

Materials You Will Need

- Bibles (preferably Common English Bible)
- Video set up to play
- Paper and writing utensils for the closing activity
- (Optional) printouts of Matthew 25:1-13 for the Extra Activity

DURING THE SESSION

Opening Activity and Prayer (6-10 minutes)

Greet folks as they arrive. In the pre-session small-talk, ask people about their families. Do your best to try to connect people who don't know each other well.

As you officially begin, explain that you're focusing on chapter 3 of *Stories Jesus Told* by Greg Carey, a book about the parables of Jesus. Encourage them to read the book on their own, chapter by chapter, week by week.

Since today's parables are both about weddings, ask the group: *Other than your own, what was the most interesting wedding you've ever attended?*

Follow up with questions that drill into the interesting factors. *What surprises occurred? How did people react?*

After a few minutes of that conversation, open the Bible-study portion of the session with prayer:

Lord, we are ready to hear from you today and learn from you. Inspire us, challenge us, teach us, grow us, as we encounter these surprising stories in your Holy Word.

Video Introduction (12 minutes)

Play the video for Session 3 of *Stories Jesus Told*.

Afterward, ask the group what they thought of the ideas presented there. What grabbed them? What was new to them? What questions do they have?

Bible Study and Book Discussion (25 minutes)

Invite the group to turn to Matthew 22 in their Bibles. (Supply Bibles or printouts to anyone who needs them.) Ask someone to read verses 1-6.

Explain that there's a parallel story in Luke 14, but Matthew's version has a number of important differences they should pay attention to. For instance, Luke has "a certain man" inviting people to a banquet, but in Matthew it's a king calling people to his son's wedding.

Point out a specific detail mentioned twice, in verses 3 and 4. Apparently the people had already been "invited," and now the servants were "calling" them to come to the wedding. Our book suggests the first invitation might have been a "save the date" sort of thing, and they were being "called" to the actual event. Ask:

- How would you respond if invited to a royal wedding?
- How did the invitees respond when they were called to come to the wedding?
- In the book, Greg Carey writes about the "hook" that most parables have—the surprise that makes it unusual. Do you see a hook (or two) in these verses?

Carey says the response was "not indifference but a direct insult." The Greek word in verse 5 indicates they "neglected, or ignored, the call to come to the party." Then, when things turn violent in verse 6, Carey notes, "We have abandoned the realm of the strange for an expedition into the truly bizarre. Surely these guests know that whoever assaults the king's enslaved servants has effectively insulted the king. Who would do that?"

Have someone read verses 7-10. Ask:

- Does the king's response surprise you? Why or why not?
- Who then gets invited to the party? What are we told about the new party guests? (Note the details that they were on "the edge of town" and "both evil and good.")
- Do you think these details are significant? Why or why not?

The violent aspects of this parable match up with the preceding story in Matthew 21, the Parable of the Tenants. Farmers renting out a vineyard kill the master's messengers and eventually even the master's son—evoking a violent response from the master. Jesus tells the religious leaders in his audience, "God's kingdom will be taken away from you and will be given to a people who produce its fruit" (Matthew 21:43). Ask:

- Do you think the original invitees to the wedding could be representing this same group—the Pharisees and religious leaders who were opposing Jesus? Why or why not?

The new invitees to the wedding party are described as "evil and good," which parallels several other parables that involve sifting—such as the Parable of the Net (Matthew 13:47-50), in which good and rotten fish are gathered up and sorted out. We may be seeing an example of this sorting in the remainder of this parable.

Have someone read verses 11-14. Ask:

- Does this surprise you?
- What do you think the wedding garment stands for?
- In our book, Greg Carey writes, "Matthew is a Gospel of surprise and insecurity." Do you see that in this parable?

when read as best in

Extra Activity (10 minutes)

If you choose not to do this activity, you may just read Matthew 25:1-13 and move to the follow-up questions. But this parable is rather simple to act out, and that might bring it to life for some group members.

A full cast would be twelve people (don't worry about gender here), but only four have speaking parts—a narrator, the groom, a spokesperson for the wise bridesmaids, and one for the foolish. (The other bridesmaids, if you have them, can murmur and ad lib.) You can easily figure out which verses should be said by which people.

If your group is active, get them standing and walking through the actions of the story (which aren't complicated). If they're sedentary, that can work too. Just seat the wise and foolish bridesmaids as groups.

Take a minute to set things up and maybe even rehearse. Then perform.

Follow-Up Questions
- How did the performers feel about this story—from the inside?
- How did the others feel as you watched your friends performing it?

- What do you think is the main lesson of this parable?
- In the book, Carey mentioned some theories about how the bridesmaids could have worked together— wise and foolish—to make it better for everyone. Does that make sense to you, or does it just distract from the main point?

Closing Activity and Prayer (8 minutes)

Read Carey's chapter conclusion to the group:

> Matthew shows us two wedding parties. Each wedding party includes the joy and wonder that accompany the kingdom of heaven. Each party invites us to marvel at the possibility that we might find ourselves included, to ponder the social event of our lives, to soak in one of the most glorious images the Gospel has to offer: celebration in the presence of Jesus. Each party also confronts us with the real possibility of exclusion. Each challenges its hearers to examine themselves, ourselves, as to whether we take our status for granted, whether we prepare appropriately, and whether we remain ready even when ordinary time seems to drag on.

Hand out index cards (or paper) and invite the group to jot down their answers to the following questions—just for themselves; they're not turning these in.

- Of the many characters in these two parables, which one do you most identify with?
- Of the different attitudes shown in these two parables, which do you want to avoid?

- What can you do to make sure you're well-prepared for Jesus' ultimate wedding party?

Then close in prayer:

Dear Lord, thank you for inviting us to your wedding party. We rely on your grace to make us ready for the joy you have in store. Give us the wisdom we need to prepare well. Amen.

Session 4

Lawyers and Samaritans

SESSION GOALS

This session aims to help group members:

- Learn the full context of the Good Samaritan parable.
- Consider their response to "Who is my neighbor?"
- Envision humble ways to give and receive love to and from others.
- Understand the assumptions of privilege in common interpretations of this parable.

BIBLICAL FOUNDATIONS

A legal expert stood up to test Jesus. "Teacher," he said, "what must I do to gain eternal life?"

Jesus replied, "What is written in the Law? How do you interpret it?"

He responded, *"You must love the Lord your God with all your heart, with all your being, with all your strength, and with all your mind, and love your neighbor as yourself."*

Jesus said to him, "You have answered correctly. Do this and you will live."

But the legal expert wanted to prove that he was right, so he said to Jesus, "And who is my neighbor?"

Jesus replied, "A man went down from Jerusalem to Jericho. He encountered thieves, who stripped him naked, beat him up, and left him near death. Now it just so happened that a priest was also going down the same road. When he saw the injured man, he crossed over to the other side of the road and went on his way. Likewise, a Levite came by that spot, saw the injured man, and crossed over to the other side of the road and went on his way. A Samaritan, who was on a journey, came to where the man was. But when he saw him, he was moved with compassion. The Samaritan went to him and bandaged his wounds, tending them with oil and wine. Then he placed the wounded man on his own donkey, took him to an inn, and took care of him. The next day, he took two full days' worth of wages and gave them to the innkeeper. He said, 'Take care of him, and when I return, I will pay you back for any additional costs.' What do you think? Which one of these three was a neighbor to the man who encountered thieves?"

Then the legal expert said, "The one who demonstrated mercy toward him."

Jesus told him, "Go and do likewise."

Luke 10:25-37

CHAPTER SUMMARY

The most common interpretation of the Good Samaritan can be dangerous.

Many use this familiar story to encourage charitable acts across cultural lines. Samaritans were despised by the Jews, and our own culture has sharp ethnic divisions as well. According to many interpreters, this parable invites us to do good to others regardless of race—or any other social prejudice.

That's dangerous because it puts us in a position of privilege, choosing the recipients of our charity. The parable places the main character—the robbery victim—in a position of need. He couldn't choose anything. He received help from the Samaritan.

Jesus told this story as part of a scholarly debate over the full scope of loving one's neighbor. The legal expert opposing Jesus was wondering who qualified as a "neighbor"—and thus a worthy recipient of his good deeds. As he often did, Jesus flipped the script with a story that challenged the man's assumptions.

Materials You Will Need

- Bibles (preferably Common English Bible)
- Video set up to play
- Paper and writing utensils for the closing activity

DURING THE SESSION

Opening Activity and Prayer (6-10 minutes)

Explain that you're focusing on chapter 4 of *Stories Jesus Told* by Greg Carey, a book about the parables of Jesus. Encourage the group to keep reading the book on their own, chapter by chapter, week by week.

Ask the group: *How well do you get along with your neighbors? Not just next-door neighbors, but others in your neighborhood? Do you have close friendships? Do you co-exist? Are there feuds?*

They don't need to share names and details but to give a sense of how people live in their neighborhoods. Be especially alert to stories of favors done for others and favors received from others. This dynamic will become important later in the session.

After a few minutes of that conversation, open the Bible-study portion of the session with prayer:

Lord, fill our hearts today as we study the Scriptures. Surprise us with new insights. Challenge our assumptions. Teach us how to love others. Amen.

Video Introduction (12 minutes)

Play the video for Session 4 of *Stories Jesus Told*.

Afterward, ask the group what they thought of the ideas presented there. What grabbed them? What was new to them? What questions do they have?

Bible Study and Book Discussion (25 minutes)

Invite the group to turn to Luke 10:25 in their Bibles. (Supply Bibles or printouts to anyone who needs them.) Ask someone to read verses 25-29.

Jesus often had discussions like this with religious experts. The Gospels record several of them. Often he was facing his enemies, and they were trying to trap him. Ask:

- What kind of encounter was this one? Do you think the man was asking an honest question, or did he have other motives?
- How did Jesus deal with this challenge?
- The man presses his case in verse 29. How would this "prove he was right" or "justify" him?

It's possible that the man was trying to prove himself as a good debater in front of his colleagues. Jesus didn't seem to be taking the bait, so the man kept pushing in an attempt to win an argument that Jesus wasn't joining. '

- The man asked, "Who is my neighbor?" What sort of answer do you think he expected?

Since he was a "legal expert," it's likely that he wanted a legal answer. He probably thought Jesus would define a neighbor as someone who lived within two miles, or someone in the same town, or any fellow Jew. Whatever he was expecting, he got more than he bargained for. Ask:

- Who is the first character we meet in this story?
- If this was a play (and don't worry—we're not acting it), which character would spend the most time on stage?
- If you were in that crowd listening to Jesus tell this story, what character would you identify with?

In the book, Carey says the answer to all those questions is "the man." The very fact that he's not further identified allows all of us (at least men) to choose him as the character we care about. The legal expert, as part of the religious elite, might wince as the priest and Levite walk on by, but even he was probably identifying with the mugging victim. Because of the bad feelings between Jews and Samaritans, he certainly would *not* see himself as the Samaritan.

Ask someone to read verses 36-37.

The legal expert had asked Jesus to define "neighbor." Jesus told this story. Now Jesus was asking the expert to answer his own question. Ask:

- How do you think the legal expert felt about that?
- Do you think there's significance in the wording of the answer he gives? (He never says the word *Samaritan*.)
- What do you think Jesus is telling the legal expert to "go and do"?
- What is he telling *us* to "go and do"?

Carey emphasizes a particular point in the book, and this may be new to some, and quite surprising.

> Over the years, I've grown convinced that our standard interpretation of the Good Samaritan parable is dangerous. That's not an exaggeration. Dangerous.

His point has to do with who is helping whom. A bit later in the book, he writes:

> A great deal of good has been accomplished under the banner of the Good Samaritan, who so often serves as our example when we perform acts of mercy. However, when we interpret the parable as a call to extend the boundaries of our charity, we place ourselves in a perilous position. We assume the chair of privilege, assuming we are the ones who will decide whether to extend help or not. Over and over again, Luke shows us what a dangerous seat that is to take. What if we find ourselves traveling down a road, beset by violent criminals and in desperate need of help? Will we be so selective about our neighbors then?

This "chair of privilege" is where the legal expert started. How many people do I have to help? He was wondering how wide to draw the circle of "neighbors" he had to show love to. But he's the one deciding whom to love. He's the one dispensing help. He sets himself on the chair of privilege and looks down on everyone else. But Jesus turns the tables. His parable "flips the script." As Carey writes:

> The parable's perspective leads us away from the perspective of privilege (the one who will save him) and into the position of vulnerability (the one who needs saving). And that is important.

Many, probably most, of the people who read the parable of the Good Samaritan see it as a challenge to help people in need—especially if they come from a downtrodden culture. While the charitable instinct is a good one—we *should* love and help others—there's a pride underlying that approach. But Jesus' story turned that around. It was the outcast who helped the man in need. As Carey writes:

> The charitable interpretation encourages readers to feel secure in our places of privilege. It aligns readers with the legal expert who asks, "Who is my neighbor?" Jesus rejects that question and the privileged subject position that it assumes. . . . [T]he lawyer wanted a neighbor in need of help, but in Jesus' parable world the neighbor is the one providing help.

Carey urges us to find that "position of vulnerability" with our neighbors. That would express the true spirit of this parable. Ask:

- How do you feel about Carey's idea that the "charitable" interpretation of this parable is "dangerous"?
- How can we find that "position of vulnerability" in our relationships?
- Can you think of particular ways we can be vulnerable in our connections with people who aren't like us?

Extra Activity (5 minutes)

This is one of the best-known stories in the Bible. If your group members are familiar with the Bible at all, they probably know this parable. So ask them to put down their Bibles or printouts or Scripture apps and just tell you the story of the Good Samaritan as they remember it.

Have fun with this, but don't put anyone on the spot—unless you know they won't mind. Try going from person to person as the story goes on. *What happened then? Who came by next?*

After they complete the story, read verses 30-35 aloud and see if you got all the details right.

Closing Activity and Prayer (10 minutes)

Divide into chat groups of three or four. Distribute index cards and pens as needed. Repeat those last two questions:

- How can we find that "position of vulnerability" in our relationships?
- Can you think of particular ways we can be vulnerable in our connections with people who aren't like us?

Give them about five minutes to brainstorm, and then ask them to share their ideas with the larger group.

Then close in prayer:

Dear Lord, we have a lot to learn about loving others. Teach us to be aware of our pride and privilege. Show us how to receive help from our neighbors. Transform us and our world in accordance with your will. Amen.

Session 5

Losing, Finding, Partying

SESSION GOALS

This session aims to help group members:

- Understand the importance Jesus placed on recovering "lost" ones.
- Experience celebration and joyous fellowship with God and others.
- Gain empathy for the characters in Jesus' parables.
- Appreciate the depth of God's love.

BIBLICAL FOUNDATIONS

All the tax collectors and sinners were gathering around Jesus to listen to him. The Pharisees and legal experts were grumbling, saying, "This man welcomes sinners and eats with them."

Jesus told them this parable: "Suppose someone among you had one hundred sheep and lost one of them. Wouldn't he leave the other ninety-nine in the pasture and search for the lost one until he finds it? And when he finds it, he is thrilled and places it on his shoulders. When he arrives home,

47

he calls together his friends and neighbors, saying to them, 'Celebrate with me because I've found my lost sheep.' In the same way, I tell you, there will be more joy in heaven over one sinner who changes both heart and life than over ninety-nine righteous people who have no need to change their hearts and lives.

"Or what woman, if she owns ten silver coins and loses one of them, won't light a lamp and sweep the house, searching her home carefully until she finds it? When she finds it, she calls together her friends and neighbors, saying, 'Celebrate with me because I've found my lost coin.' In the same way, I tell you, joy breaks out in the presence of God's angels over one sinner who changes both heart and life."

Jesus said, "A certain man had two sons. The younger son said to his father, 'Father, give me my share of the inheritance.' Then the father divided his estate between them. Soon afterward, the younger son gathered everything together and took a trip to a land far away. There, he wasted his wealth through extravagant living.

"When he had used up his resources, a severe food shortage arose in that country and he began to be in need. He hired himself out to one of the citizens of that country, who sent him into his fields to feed pigs. He longed to eat his fill from what the pigs ate, but no one gave him anything. When he came to his senses, he said, 'How many of my father's hired hands have more than enough food, but I'm starving to death! I will get up and go to my father, and say to him, "Father, I have sinned against heaven and against you. I no longer deserve to be called your son. Take me on as one of your hired hands."' So he got up and went to his father.

"While he was still a long way off, his father saw him and was moved with compassion. His father ran to him, hugged him, and kissed him. Then his son said, 'Father, I have sinned against heaven and against you. I no longer deserve to be called your son.' But the father said to his servants, 'Quickly, bring out the best robe and put it on him! Put a ring on his finger and sandals on his feet! Fetch the fattened calf and slaughter it. We must celebrate with feasting because this son of mine was dead and has come back to life! He was lost and is found!' And they began to celebrate.

"Now his older son was in the field. Coming in from the field, he approached the house and heard music and dancing. He called one of the servants and asked what was going on. The servant replied, 'Your brother has arrived, and your father has slaughtered the fattened calf because he received his son back safe and sound.' Then the older son was furious and didn't want to enter in, but his father came out and begged him. He answered his father, 'Look, I've served you all these years, and I never disobeyed your instruction. Yet you've never given me as much as a young goat so I could celebrate with my friends. But when this son of yours returned, after gobbling up your estate on prostitutes, you slaughtered the fattened calf for him.' Then his father said, 'Son, you are always with me, and everything I have is yours. But we had to celebrate and be glad because this brother of yours was dead and is alive. He was lost and is found.'"

Luke 15:1-32

CHAPTER SUMMARY

Masterfully, Luke sets the scene for this collection of parables. As we see throughout Jesus' ministry, he is connecting with "sinners"—people who have been excluded by the religious leaders. Jesus responds to the carping of those leaders with three parables about finding what's lost.

A shepherd loses a sheep; a woman loses a coin. They search exhaustively and finally find what they've lost. Then they invite their neighbors to a celebratory party. (It's no surprise that Luke writes about gatherings that include food. It's common for him, and it seems to be Jesus' style.)

The third parable extends the same pattern, only this time

a man loses his son. For the first time, we get into the mind of the lost one, and we see his decision to return. The father is waiting, welcoming him with open arms. And of course, there's a party.

But this third parable adds a new character, an older son who's not part of this welcome-back party. In a complaint that mirrors what Jesus' critics have been saying, the older son protests that he has always been loyal and faithful—so what's all the fuss about this errant boy?

Luke loves to emphasize the crisis situations that people face. Several parables in this Gospel hinge on life-changing events or crucial decisions. The Prodigal Son story shows us three people in crisis mode. How do they handle it?

Materials You Will Need

- Bibles (preferably Common English Bible)
- Video set up to play
- Paper and writing utensils for the closing activity

DURING THE SESSION

Opening Activity and Prayer (6-10 minutes)

Since today's parables are about lost things, ask the group: *What have you lost recently and later found? Your keys, cell phone, a piece of jewelry, a credit card, a favorite sweatshirt?*

Follow up with questions like: *How did you feel when you couldn't find this? How did you feel when you found it? Did you tell anybody, call anybody, reward yourself?*

After a few minutes of that conversation, open the Bible-study portion of the session with prayer:

Lord, the stories we read in the Gospels are like the stories of our lives. We encounter ordinary things and common relationships, but you always take us deeper, to the core of who we are and who you are. Keep teaching us as we come before your word today. Amen.

Video Introduction (12 minutes)

Play the video for Session 5 of *Stories Jesus Told*.

Afterward, ask the group what they thought of the ideas presented there. What grabbed them? What was new to them? What questions do they have?

Bible Study and Book Discussion (25 minutes)

Invite the group to turn to Luke 15 in their Bibles. (Supply Bibles or printouts to anyone who needs them.) Ask someone to read verses 1-2.

Before you start asking questions, explain that this chapter is a work of art. There's a clear structure, compelling characters, and a theme that builds. We'll gather some deep spiritual lessons from these parables but also take a moment to appreciate the literary merit of this collection.

That artistry starts with the opening snapshot. Ask:

- Who's present as Jesus tells these stories?
- What's the dynamic? What are these people doing, thinking, saying?

Have someone read verses 3-10. These are two different stories about things lost and found. Ask:

- What's different about these two stories?
- What do these two stories have in common?

- In both stories, what happens after they find what was lost?
- After each parable, Jesus gives a similar statement about sinners repenting. What do sinners have to do with a sheep or a coin?

Those are the opening acts. Now we get to the main event. The Parable of the Prodigal Son is one of the best-known stories in the Bible. This means we have all heard a lot of preachers tell the story in their own ways. It always helps to come back to the source. Have someone read verses 11-16. Ask:

- What subtitle would you give to this part of the story?
- Are there any details you wish you knew, but the story doesn't provide?
- How would you describe the younger son's situation at the end of verse 16?

Have someone read verses 17-24. Note that one feature of Luke's parables is that we can sometimes hear what characters are thinking. That happens here in the pigsty as the son rehearses what to say to his father. A few verses later he says the same thing out loud . . . almost. Ask:

- What part of his rehearsed speech does he skip when he speaks to his father? Why?
- There's a beautiful detail in the middle of verse 20. What does this say about what the father was doing while his son was gone? [Father saw him "a long way off."]
- What words would you use to describe the father's attitude at his son's return?
- How does this story, so far, compare with the stories of the sheep and the coin? What's similar? What's different?

While the parables of the lost sheep and lost coin end with the finding and the party, this story has a final act. Let's hear it. Have someone read verses 25-32. Ask:

- What's your impression of the older son? Why?

Here's what Greg Carey writes about him:

> Despite his lack of charity, I sympathize with the old brother on one key point. Certainly he is correct about one thing: the younger brother has just wasted one-third of the household's resources, yet he is welcomed with a party. All the more galling, though, the older son remains in the field while the party takes off. No one, it seems, has bothered to look for him—and that includes his father. So familiar is this parable to many of us that we overlook this crucial detail. The older son finds out about the party by *hearing* the music and dancing. He is reduced to asking a slave what is going on.

- Does that change your opinion at all?
- Remember that Jesus was talking to a mixed group of "sinners" and religious leaders. Do you think they would see themselves in certain characters of this story?

Often we come at Jesus' parables looking for definitive answers. We want solid answers to what these stories mean. But maybe there are other ways to treat these parables, as Carey suggests in the following selection:

> Jesus' parables prefer to provoke our curiosity rather than to satisfy it. They leave gaps unexplained. I'd like to know *why* this younger son wanted to set off on his own, wouldn't you? It

can be a healthy discipline *not* to pursue that line of curiosity, to allow the parable to set its own terms and hold our curiosity at bay. Certainly we should not impose our assumptions upon the story and read it as if we know what's on this young man's mind. Parables call for curiosity and wonder. They are not ours to control.

But a disciplined curiosity can be a good thing. If we can hold our questions loosely, suggesting possibilities rather than committing ourselves to just one option, it might be helpful to brainstorm the range of options. Perhaps the younger son is simply foolish; being young and inexperienced, he has no idea what he's getting into, and his youthful desire for adventure out-strips his judgment. His behavior suggests that may be the case, as he clearly has no sustainabil-ity plan for making his share of the inheritance last. But should we close off the possibility that something is pushing the younger son to leave home, either something inside himself or some-thing wrong in the family dynamics? Without committing ourselves to an explanation, it may be good to remember that we do not know why the young man leaves home.

- What do you think of this? Do you agree? Disagree? Why?
- What is "disciplined curiosity"? How do you think we could "hold our questions loosely"?
- This quote uses the example of the Prodigal Son, but are there other parables we've studied that could use some of this "disciplined curiosity" rather than defini-tive interpretations? Like what?

Closing Activity and Prayer (10 minutes)

"Luke is fond of crisis parables," Carey writes. We often see characters at a point of decision, or need, or change.

Hand out cards and writing utensils and invite people to think about their own crisis moments. The cards are only for their own use, to jot down thoughts that come to mind. Ask them to think about these questions:

Which of the characters in Luke 15 do you identify with? The shepherd, the woman who lost the coin, the father, or one of the two sons? Or perhaps one of these characters reminds you of someone you know and care about.

What can you learn from these parables? Do you need to keep looking? Do you need to come home? Do you need to throw a party? Do you need to reconsider your bitterness?

Close in prayer, possibly using these words:

Our loving God, we live in a lost-and-found world. It's easy to lose our way, to grab what we think we deserve and wander away from you. It's easy to be bitter about the joys of others. It's easy to lose heart, to lose hope. Guide us home, we pray. Show us the way back into your joyous presence. Amen.

Session 6

A Reversal of Fortune

SESSION GOALS

This session aims to help group members:

- Understand the main themes of the Parable of the Rich Man and Lazarus.
- Consider what the parable teaches (or doesn't teach) about the afterlife.
- Evaluate their own response to the poor.
- Learn about Luke's interest in "turnabout" of privilege in society.

BIBLICAL FOUNDATIONS

"There was a certain rich man who clothed himself in purple and fine linen, and who feasted luxuriously every day. At his gate lay a certain poor man named Lazarus who was covered with sores. Lazarus longed to eat the crumbs that fell from the rich man's table. Instead, dogs would come and lick his sores.

"The poor man died and was carried by angels to Abraham's side. The rich man also died and was buried. While being tormented in the place of the dead, he looked up and saw Abraham at a distance with Lazarus at his side. He shouted, 'Father Abraham, have mercy on me. Send Lazarus to dip the tip of his finger in water and cool my tongue, because I'm suffering in this flame.' But Abraham said, 'Child, remember that during your lifetime you received good things, whereas Lazarus received terrible things. Now Lazarus is being comforted and you are in great pain. Moreover, a great crevasse has been fixed between us and you. Those who wish to cross over from here to you cannot. Neither can anyone cross from there to us.'

"The rich man said, 'Then I beg you, Father, send Lazarus to my father's house. I have five brothers. He needs to warn them so that they don't come to this place of agony.' Abraham replied, 'They have Moses and the Prophets. They must listen to them.' The rich man said, 'No, Father Abraham! But if someone from the dead goes to them, they will change their hearts and lives.' Abraham said, 'If they don't listen to Moses and the Prophets, then neither will they be persuaded if someone rises from the dead.'"

Luke 16:19-31

CHAPTER SUMMARY

After two well-known and well-loved parables (the Good Samaritan and the Prodigal Son), we come to a lesser-known one, the Rich Man and Lazarus. Perhaps this story bothers us because it challenges our theology of salvation, heaven, and wealth.

Luke often depicts characters in crisis, and this is another great example. The rich man dies and is forced to see the results of his self-centered indifference. This parable also demonstrates Luke's interest in social reversal. We see that in the way Jesus treats women, "sinners," and Samaritans. Here we see the rich and the poor switching status in the world to come.

We can learn from all these themes, and we should certainly be on the lookout for self-centered indifference in our own lives, but it's a tough story on which to build a theology of heaven.

Materials You Will Need

- Bibles (preferably Common English Bible)
- Video set up to play
- Paper and writing utensils for the closing activity

DURING THE SESSION

Opening Activity and Prayer (8-12 minutes)

Explain that this is the final session of the study on *Stories Jesus Told* by Greg Carey. (You may want to preview what's next for your group.)

Ask the group: *What have you been learning here about Jesus' parables? Have you gained any new insights? Do you understand them any differently?* (As the leader, be ready with your own answers to those questions.)

After a few minutes of that conversation, open the Bible-study portion of the session with prayer:

Lord, speak to us again today through your word. We open our lives to your gaze and your guidance. Challenge us where we need challenging. Bolster us where we need bolstering. Teach us today, we pray. Amen.

Video Introduction (12 minutes)

Play the video for Session 6 of *Stories Jesus Told*.

Afterward, ask the group what they thought of the ideas

presented there. What grabbed them? What was new to them? What questions do they have?

Bible Study and Book Discussion (25 minutes)

Invite the group to turn to Luke 16:19 in their Bibles. (Supply Bibles or printouts to anyone who needs them.) Ask someone to read verses 19-21.

Before digging into this text, pause to marvel at the writing of it. In just three verses—less than sixty words—we are given a vivid picture of how two men lived their lives. Ask:

- What details strike you about this picture?
- What was the connection between these two men?
- According to these verses, was the rich man doing anything sinful?

That's an interesting question. Is it wrong to feast while someone is at your gate starving? In the book, Carey mentions sins of "omission." Maybe the neglect of this beggar was not wrong-doing, but ignoring an obligation for right-doing.

Ask someone to read verses 22-26. Acknowledge that these verses give us a view of the afterlife that we're not used to. Read this excerpt from Carey's book:

> Luke uses some terminology that may give us pause. The Rich Man goes to *Hades,* which is a place of torment. The angels carry Lazarus to *Abraham's bosom.* And Jesus promises *paradise* to his crucified neighbor. None of these terms corresponds precisely to our common notions of heaven and hell. Hades is taken from Greek cosmology, a realm of the dead that could include places of punishment *and* places of blessing. The precise meaning of Abraham's bosom is less

clear. Paradise is likewise unknown. One ancient Jewish text may provide some help. The *Testament of Abraham* depicts Abraham in paradise. There the righteous dwell, with Isaac and Jacob residing in Abraham's bosom. In that place there is no labor, no grief, and no mourning but peace and exaltation and eternal life (20:14).

- Do you think this parable is (a) teaching us what the afterlife is like or (b) using common ideas of that time to tell a story about rich and poor men or (c) both?
- The parable presents the idea that there is communication between the two sides of the afterlife—even though there's a crevasse preventing travel between them. What does the rich man say, and to whom does he speak?
- Why do you think he does not address Lazarus directly?

Carey suggests that the rich man still sees Lazarus as an underling, someone that "Father Abraham" would send on an errand. This exchange indicates that he knew who Lazarus was, though maybe he had never talked to him. Ask:

- How does Abraham respond to the rich man?
- Do you think Abraham is teaching an important principle about life in this world and the next?

Have someone read verses 27-31. Ask:

- What's the message that the rich man wants to send to his brothers?
- Why does Abraham reject that request?
- Ultimately the problem for the rich man and his brothers is *not* a lack of information. What *is* the problem?

Carey mentions three problems people have with this parable. We've already talked about the first: its picture of heaven goes against what many people believe. The second problem is this matter of "Moses and the prophets," and particularly the keeping of the Old Testament law as one's ticket to heaven. Doesn't Paul say we're justified by faith?

But Carey goes on to say this:

> The Parable of the Rich Man and Lazarus does raise questions of justification and the afterlife, but it remains a parable. We should take caution not to push the parable too far on either issue. We should be even *more* cautious, however, not to dismiss it. There's a sweet spot somewhere between turning a parable into a doctrinal statement and ignoring the issues it addresses. I recommend taking the parable seriously—and holding our judgments lightly. Luke is serious about the afterlife. Pointedly, Luke links our afterlife hope with how we relate to the poor.

That leads us to the third issue: many of us are uneasy about our own relationship to money and treatment of the poor. Here's how Carey puts it:

> According to Luke, one category of sin does hold Jesus' attention: self-centered indifference, or knowing about the needs of others and not caring. Jesus never names this sin, but it manifests itself throughout the Gospel. The Parable of the Rich Man and Lazarus constitutes Exhibit A of this pattern. Lazarus lies destitute, hungry and in pain, while the Rich Man goes on with his feasting. As the parable develops, we learn that the Rich Man knew about Lazarus all along, for he recognizes his poor neighbor in the afterlife.

He even desires that Lazarus run his errands!
The Rich Man sins not in being rich but in ne-
glecting the need of his neighbor.

. . . When people are more concerned with
their own affairs than with the things of God
and the needs of others, they fail to follow Jesus
(9:57-62; 14:15-24). Self-centered indifference
poses a grave spiritual danger. It poses as taking care of one's own business, but it prevents
people from tending to things more essential
(21:34). This may account for Jesus' saying it is
"very hard" for the rich to enter God's kingdom
(18:24-25).

- Do you feel the phrase "self-centered indifference"
  accurately captures the attitude of the rich man in this
  story?
- Do you think self-centered indifference is a problem
  among Christians today?
- If so, what can be done about it?

Closing Activity and Prayer (10 minutes)

Distribute cards and pens as usual. As before, these are for
personal note-taking, jotting down whatever the Lord brings
to mind.

There are several confusing things about the parable of
the Rich Man and Lazarus, but the takeaway is crystal clear:
Don't be that guy! As Greg Carey has identified the problem,
we should all seek to avoid "self-centered indifference."
Maybe there are beggars at our door that we've never paid
attention to.

Ask the group to pay attention now. Take these next
few moments in prayer, perhaps confessing sins of omission,

perhaps committing to acts of compassion, perhaps prying open our eyes to see the needs around us.

As the leader, talk them through this process. Suggest different needs they might look for, as well as different ways to help. Perhaps your community has people like Lazarus, very needy people who beg on the street. How can you help? What kinds of needs are visible or invisible in your community? (Maybe you, as the leader, can add particular needs and ministries of your church.)

After a suitable time, close in prayer:

Eternal God, open our eyes to see the neighbors who need your love, expressed through us. Give us courage to act, compassion to drive us, wisdom to do it well, and a willingness to be vulnerable. We're sorry for past self-centeredness and indifference. Open us to the needs around us, so we may humbly serve you. Amen.

CPSIA information can be obtained
at www.ICGtesting.com
Printed in the USA
LVHW021916110619
620906LV00001B/2